Original title:
Healing Together

Copyright © 2024 Swan Charm
All rights reserved.

Author: Paulina Pähkel
ISBN HARDBACK: 978-9916-79-147-9
ISBN PAPERBACK: 978-9916-79-148-6
ISBN EBOOK: 978-9916-79-149-3

The Circle of Unity

In the dawn's gentle light, we gather as one,
Hands raised in prayer, our hearts weigh the sun.
Voices blend softly, like rivers' sweet flow,
In the circle of unity, love's seeds we sow.

Beneath the vast sky, a tapestry bright,
Each thread represents dreams, woven in light.
With faith as our anchor, we stand side by side,
We're branches of one tree, with roots deep and wide.

As seasons will change, our spirits will grow,
With kindness and grace, we nurture the glow.
In trials and triumphs, we journey as friends,
In the circle of unity, love never ends.

The whispers of ancients, the wisdom they share,
Remind us of journeys, of burdens we bear.
Through storms that may rage, our hearts stay aligned,
In the circle of unity, peace we will find.

So gather, dear kin, let our voices ascend,
In harmony singing, our spirits we mend.
For life is a circle, where souls intertwine,
In the circle of unity, your heart beats with mine.

A Pilgrimage of the Heart

With each step I take, my heart begins to soar,
Through valleys of silence, to the open door.
In whispers of wisdom, the sacred I find,
On a pilgrimage of the heart, my spirit unconfined.

The mountains stand tall, guardians of the way,
Their shadows embrace me at the break of day.
With faith as my compass, I follow the call,
On this journey of truth, I rise each time I fall.

As rivers flow onward, so does my desire,
To seek out the knowledge that lifts me higher.
In every reflection, in every sweet art,
I gather the pieces, a pilgrimage of the heart.

In gardens of plenty, where flowers all bloom,
I pause to remember the light in the gloom.
With gratitude flowing, I cherish each part,
As I walk through the ages, a pilgrimage of the heart.

Thus, I travel onward, with love as my guide,
Through the storms and the stillness, in joy I abide.
For the path is the making, the journey, a start,
On this endless pilgrimage, the essence is heart.

Anointing of Togetherness

In the light we gather here,
With hearts as one, we shed our fear.
In praise we lift our voices high,
Embracing love that will not die.

Each hand in hand, we build the way,
Through trials dark, we shall not sway.
With faith infused in every prayer,
Together strong, we rise and share.

Anointing hope, our spirits glow,
In unity, the seeds we sow.
With every step, a bond refined,
In sacred space, our souls aligned.

Let kindness flow, a gentle stream,
In every heart, we weave our dream.
Through grace divine, our paths are blessed,
In togetherness, we find our rest.

The Fellowship of Resilience

In shadows cast, we stand as one,
With hearts ablaze, our fight begun.
Through storms we face, we know no fear,
In fellowship, our strength is clear.

Each struggle bold, a story told,
Of courage fierce, of spirits gold.
In trials deep, we find our song,
Through every tear, we still belong.

Together we will rise again,
With faith unyielding, through the pain.
In bonds of trust, our hearts ignite,
A fellowship that brings the light.

Let every voice in harmony,
Echo the truth of unity.
In shared belief, we stand as one,
Together strong, till day is done.

A Journey of Renewal

In whispered prayer, a journey starts,
With open minds and seeking hearts.
Through winding paths, we seek the true,
In every step, a grace anew.

With every dawn, the light unfolds,
In sacred trust, a tale retold.
Through trials faced, we shed the past,
Renewed in spirit, free at last.

Each moment blessed, a gift we share,
In every breath, we find our prayer.
The road ahead, we walk with grace,
In journey's light, we find our place.

Together we shall learn and grow,
In love's embrace, the world we know.
With open hearts, the future bright,
A journey blessed, in faith and light.

The Gentle Embrace of Unity

In stillness found, we gather near,
With gentle hearts, we cast our fear.
In unity, the world we form,
Through love's embrace, we weather storm.

Each voice a thread in woven grace,
In harmony, we find our space.
With kindness sown in every deed,
Together strong, we plant the seed.

Through varied paths, we walk as one,
In shared belief, our work begun.
With open arms, we share the load,
In gentle hands, love's seed is sowed.

In every heart, a flame ignites,
In unity, we reach new heights.
The ties that bind, forever strong,
In gentle embrace, we all belong.

Divine Mendings

In whispers soft, He heals the soul,
With tender grace, He makes us whole.
Through trials faced and burdens borne,
In faith restored, new hope is worn.

His love a balm for wounds that bleed,
In every heart, a quiet creed.
With hands outstretched, He mends the tears,
A testament to how He cares.

From shattered dreams, new paths arise,
By sacred light, we learn to rise.
In gentle night, His presence glows,
With every step, His guidance shows.

Together bound by holy ties,
We find our strength, the spirit flies.
In every prayer, His promise rings,
The joy that faith in Love now brings.

When Hearts Intertwine

Two souls entwined beneath the sky,
In sacred dance, our spirits fly.
With every glance, a silent vow,
In love's embrace, we anchor now.

Through trials faced, together stand,
In light of grace, we hold His hand.
With whispers sweet, our hearts remain,
In joy and pain, we share the strain.

A tapestry of faith and trust,
In every thread, our hearts adjust.
A guiding hope in each embrace,
In found redemption, we seek grace.

With kindness sown, our days unfold,
In stories shared, we find the gold.
In every heartbeat, love's refrain,
A promise kept, like gentle rain.

In the Shadow of His Wings

In quiet night, with stars alight,
We find our peace in holy sight.
Beneath His wings, we seek our rest,
In solace found, our hearts are blessed.

The storms may rise, we shall not fear,
For in His love, He draws us near.
With each soft breath, we feel His grace,
In every moment, we find our place.

He shelters us through darkest days,
With gentle hands, in myriad ways.
His promises a shining guide,
In every tear, He stands beside.

Our faith, a light that never wanes,
In joy and sorrow, love remains.
In shadows deep, His truth reveals,
The tender love that always heals.

Serenity in Communion

In quiet gatherings, hearts align,
In sacred space, our souls entwine.
With open hands, we share the love,
A hymn of hope that sings above.

In prayerful whispers, we unite,
With faith ablaze, we seek the light.
Through laughter shared and tears esteemed,
In every moment, grace redeemed.

Together we walk the narrow path,
In unity found, we share His wrath.
Each story told, a step we take,
In love's embrace, our hearts awake.

With every breath, we feel His peace,
In holy bond, our cares release.
With hearts aglow, we find our way,
In sacred union, come what may.

Embracing the Divine Together

In the stillness of prayer, we meet,
Hearts entwined, our souls complete.
With faith as our guiding star,
Together, we journey near and far.

In the warmth of each other's embrace,
We find solace in divine grace.
Through trials, our spirits soar,
United, we seek forevermore.

With whispers of hope, we grow,
In sacred circles, love will flow.
Hand in hand, our voices rise,
As heaven opens, the heart replies.

In moments of joy, or despair,
We share burdens, we deeply care.
In prayer's quiet strength, we stand,
Together, we hold the Creator's hand.

Through valleys low, and mountains high,
Together we search, together we cry.
In faith's embrace, we feel alive,
With each heartbeat, our spirits thrive.

The Bond of Shared Burdens

In shadows cast by doubt and fear,
We bear each other, always near.
With every trial, a lesson learned,
The fire of our faith is truly burned.

With hands together, we pave the way,
For love will guide us, come what may.
In the struggle, we find our strength,
Together, we journey any length.

As we lift the weight of despair,
In communion, we breathe the prayer.
Moments shared in silent peace,
Through love, our burdens find release.

Each tear shed is a gift divine,
In unity's glow, our spirits shine.
Bound by faith, we'll never fall,
Our hearts are lifted, one and all.

Together we carry the world's plight,
With compassion's glow, we ignite.
In every sigh, in every laugh,
With shared burdens, we find our path.

Walking the Path of Mercy

With gentle steps in the light we tread,
In mercy's embrace, our hearts are led.
Through every shadow, we seek the dawn,
In the name of love, we journey on.

With open hearts, we extend our hands,
For mercy speaks in the quiet lands.
In kindness shared, spirits renew,
The path we walk is ever true.

Forgiveness whispered in the night,
As we shine together, a guiding light.
With every heartbeat, we choose to heal,
In mercy's name, we make the deal.

Through trials faced, we rise anew,
In every act of grace, we pursue.
With every tear, joy has a place,
United in love, we find our grace.

Through the storms of life, we stand,
Walking together, hand in hand.
In compassion's glow, we find our way,
With mercy's hope, we greet the day.

Echoes of Love and Faith

In the silence, love's soft call,
Echoes through the hearts of all.
With faith as our anchor, we rise,
Together, we touch the skies.

From the depths of our souls, we sing,
In joyous harmony, blessings spring.
With every note, our spirits blend,
In love and faith, we find a friend.

Through valleys of doubt, we wander wide,
With hope as our lantern, we turn the tide.
In each other's arms, our fears release,
In echoes of love, we find our peace.

With every story, our hearts unfold,
In whispered dreams, a truth retold.
In faith's embrace, we stand so tall,
Together we answer the sacred call.

As we gather, our voices rise,
In love's embrace, we realize.
With echoes of faith, our journey blends,
In every heartbeat, love transcends.

Light Through Shared Trials

In shadows deep, we walk as one,
With faith as our guide, we rise from the done.
Through trials faced, our spirits shine,
Together we stand, your heart in mine.

With whispered prayers, we find our way,
In stormy nights, the dawn will sway.
Each tear we shed, a testament true,
Reflects the light, in me, in you.

Though burdens weigh, we're never alone,
In love's embrace, our seeds are sown.
From ashes of worry, hope will bloom,
Hand in hand, we'll banish the gloom.

Let kindness flow, a river wide,
In this sacred space, we abide.
With every step on this shared road,
Together, we lighten each heavy load.

The Garden of Rebirth

In fields of grace, new life will grow,
Where faith is planted, love will sow.
From darkened soil, a flower will rise,
Unveiling petals 'neath radiant skies.

With every season, the earth renews,
The spirit dances, in vibrant hues.
From winter's chill, the warmth will come,
In nature's arms, our hearts are numb.

The whispers of spring, a sweet refrain,
In moments of loss, we find our gain.
Each bud unfurling tells a story,
Of trials faced, and hidden glory.

Embrace the sun, let shadows flee,
In this garden, we're truly free.
As life entwines, we learn to see,
The beauty found in just being we.

Threads of Mercy

In tapestry woven, our lives entwined,
Threads of mercy, gently aligned.
Each act of grace, a stitch with care,
A sacred bond, a light we share.

With every kindness, the fabric grows,
In the loom of love, the spirit flows.
Through trials faced, our hearts expand,
As gentle hands meet, we understand.

In moments of doubt, when shadows creep,
We find the strength, our promise to keep.
Each thread of hope, a shimmering strand,
In the grand design, we take our stand.

Together we weave, a tapestry bright,
In love's embrace, we find our light.
With every prayer, our voices blend,
Sharing mercy, until the end.

Revelations of the Spirit

In silence, we hear the spirit's call,
Whispers of wisdom, enchanting us all.
Through quiet reflection, our hearts become clear,
Revelations unfold, drawing us near.

In moments of stillness, the truth ignites,
Guiding our souls through the darkest nights.
With each gentle nudge, the spirit does steer,
Awakening dreams that once felt so dear.

Like soft gentle breezes, insights arrive,
Inviting our hearts, reminding us to thrive.
In sacred communion, we are reborn,
Guided by love every day, every morn.

With openness wide, we embrace the unknown,
In the dance of life's rhythm, we find our own tone.
Let revelations soar, our spirits take flight,
In this journey of faith, we bask in the light.

In the Embrace of the Eternal

In the silence of prayer, we meet,
Hearts entwined, our souls take flight.
Guided by faith, we seek the light,
In the embrace of the Eternal's sweet.

Waves of grace surround our being,
In every whisper, His love we find.
Every tear shed, a path to healing,
In sacred stillness, our hearts aligned.

Under stars that brightly shimmer,
We gather close, sharing our fears.
In moments of doubt, our spirits glimmer,
Together we'll conquer, through all the years.

His voice in the wind, gentle and clear,
Calls us forth to serve with love.
In the warmth of His presence, cast out fear,
United we journey, guided from above.

As one we rise, as one we stand,
In the tapestry woven by divine thread.
With faith as our beacon, hand in hand,
In the embrace of the Eternal, we are led.

Communal Solace

In the circle of grace, we gather near,
Words of comfort, wisdom shared.
Voices blended, dispelling fear,
In communal solace, our hearts are bared.

Through trials faced, together we stand,
Lifting each other in love's embrace.
In unity forged by God's own hand,
We find our strength in this sacred space.

Beneath the vast and watchful sky,
We lift our prayers as one, in trust.
With each shared moment, we learn to fly,
In the bonds of faith, we are robust.

Hope ignites like a radiant flame,
In the hearts of those who dare to dream.
With love as our anchor, we call His name,
In communal solace, we find our theme.

Together we walk this winding road,
Each step a testament to our belief.
In shared burdens, our hearts are owed,
In communal solace, we find relief.

The Strength of Our Brotherhood

In the forge of trials, we are molded,
Beneath the burden, our spirits rise.
With courage sown and love unfolded,
The strength of our brotherhood defies.

Hand in hand through storms we tread,
Each challenge met with faith renewed.
In unity's grip, no fear, no dread,
The strength of our brotherhood is viewed.

Voices united, our prayers ignite,
In harmony, we find our way.
With hearts ablaze, we seek the light,
The strength of our brotherhood will stay.

Every struggle binds us tight,
In shared hope, we boldly strive.
Through darkest nights, we see the light,
The strength of our brotherhood alive.

As brothers forged in the fires of grace,
We rise together, and never fall.
In the love we share, we find our place,
The strength of our brotherhood stands tall.

Beacon of Collective Faith

In the shadows deep, our light will shine,
A beacon bright in the night's embrace.
With open hearts, our spirits align,
A beacon of collective faith, our grace.

Sowing seeds of hope in barren lands,
Together we flourish, side by side.
In every effort, God's gentle hands,
A beacon of collective faith as our guide.

When doubts arise, and fears take hold,
We gather strength, our voices lift.
In unity's chorus, both fierce and bold,
A beacon of collective faith, our gift.

Together we rise, refusing to break,
In every challenge, we find our way.
With love as our anchor, for His name's sake,
A beacon of collective faith, we pray.

As we journey forth, let kindness reign,
In our hearts, truth's light must stay.
With faith unyielding, we'll break every chain,
A beacon of collective faith, come what may.

Of One Heart and Spirit

In the silence, we gather near,
Voices whisper, filled with cheer.
Hands united, we stand tall,
In love's embrace, we shall not fall.

Faith a beacon, shining bright,
Guiding us through the darkest night.
With every prayer, our spirits rise,
Reaching hearts, touching skies.

Together we walk this sacred ground,
In harmony's dance, we are found.
Each step a testament, strong and clear,
Of one heart and spirit, we persevere.

In the light of grace, we find our way,
Through trials faced, come what may.
Together, woven in divine thread,
Living truth in each word said.

As we journey, hand in hand,
We become the light across the land.
In unity, our purpose brought,
By love and faith, we are taught.

Reflections in the Holy Waters

By the river, calm and deep,
Secrets of silence in shadows creep.
Rippling visions of what will be,
Reflections of grace, calling me.

In stillness, I find my peace,
From burdens heavy, I seek release.
The water's whispers, soft as breath,
In every wave, a dance with death.

Cleansed by waters, sacred and free,
I surrender my soul, to simply be.
Each droplet carries a story of old,
In the current, my spirit feels bold.

Beneath the surface, I peer within,
Finding the light that heals my sin.
In holy waters, I'm reborn once more,
A spirit untamed, to freely soar.

From the depths, I rise anew,
With every ripple, my heart beats true.
Reflections in time, a journey begun,
In sacred waters, we are one.

The Tuning of Souls

In the quiet, hearts align,
Resonating with the divine.
Each note we share, a prayer refined,
In harmony, our spirits intertwined.

With every word, a melody flows,
In sacred space, the music grows.
Voices lifted, breaking the night,
In the symphony of love, we find light.

As strings are plucked, each soul reacts,
In this orchestra, no one lacks.
Together, we create a tune,
A chorus of hope, beneath the moon.

Moments meld, like woven thread,
In the tapestry of life, we tread.
The tuning of souls, a sacred art,
In life's grand song, we're never apart.

So let us play, with hearts ablaze,
In unity, through all our days.
For in this music, we find our goal,
A sweet serenade, the tuning of souls.

A Symphony of Survival

In the shadows, we find our strength,
Journeyed far, at great length.
Each struggle faced, a note sublime,
Composing life's rhythm, in challenging times.

Through valleys deep and mountains high,
We rise again, reaching for the sky.
With courage fierce, we stand our ground,
In the symphony of survival, hope is found.

Together we dance, in trials and tears,
Holding each other through our fears.
Every heartbeat, a pulse of grace,
In unison, we grow, we embrace.

In storms that rage and winds that blow,
Our spirits entwine, together we grow.
Strumming the chords of life's sweet song,
In the symphony of survival, we belong.

So let the music of life play on,
With every dawn, a chance reborn.
In this orchestra, we shall thrive,
For in togetherness, we are alive.

Journey to Wholeness

In stillness, prayer whispers soft,
Hearts open wide to the divine call.
With every step, faith lifts us up,
Embracing light, we rise from our fall.

Grace interweaves through each heart's strain,
Wounds transformed into sacred art.
In surrender, we find the power,
United, we heal, we grow, we start.

Through valleys deep, our spirits soar,
In unity, we gather strength anew.
Each trial builds a bridge to peace,
With love as our guide, we break through.

In humble service, we find our way,
Together, we journey, hand in hand.
Each moment a gift, each breath a prayer,
Walking forth on holy, sacred land.

As we reach for the eternal light,
Our lives a song of harmonized grace.
With souls aligned, we shine together,
In wholeness, we find our lasting place.

Together in Holy Refuge

In twilight's glow, we seek your face,
A shelter from the storms of strife.
With open hearts and whispered hopes,
We find our way to sacred life.

Bound by love, our spirits rise,
In unity, we gather as one.
A refuge built on faith's embrace,
In your presence, our hearts become undone.

Through laughter shared and tears that flow,
In every moment, your grace we see.
Together, we weave a tapestry,
Of prayers spoken, wild and free.

In quiet corners, where love abides,
We share our burdens, ease our pain.
Each story told, a blessing shared,
In holy refuge, we rise again.

With every breath, we seek to know,
The beauty found in hearts entwined.
Together we lift our voices high,
In sacred trust, our souls are aligned.

The Tapestry of Souls

Threads of light in colors bright,
Weaving stories of love untold.
In every heart, a sacred spark,
Together, we shine, we break the mold.

Life's rich fabric, textured and deep,
Every thread holds a tale to share.
In patience and grace, we find our way,
Each knot a moment, precious and rare.

With hands combined, we stitch our dreams,
Creating patterns that sing and dance.
In this tapestry, our spirits blend,
A beautiful collage, a sacred romance.

Through trials that stretch, we learn to grow,
With gratitude stitched into each seam.
In the loom of faith, our stories bind,
A masterpiece formed from love's sweet dream.

Together as one, our hearts shall soar,
In the tapestry of souls we find,
A vision of hope, a mission of grace,
For in unity, our spirits are aligned.

Pilgrims on a Shared Path

On this journey, hand in hand,
We walk beneath the watchful skies.
Each step a prayer, each breath a vow,
As seekers, we rise to the light that lies.

With humble hearts, we tread this road,
Learning wisdom from storms and sun.
In the footprints left by those before,
We find our stride, our race begun.

Through winding trails and sacred sights,
Pilgrims on a quest to behold.
In the unity of our purpose strong,
We gather stories, both new and old.

With every sharing, our burdens lighten,
In every laughter, love is seen.
Together we carry each other's hopes,
Binding our hearts in the shared unseen.

As we wander to places unknown,
With faith our compass, we shall roam.
For together, we find our sacred ground,
In every heart, we find a home.

Restoration Through Faith

In shadows deep, our spirits cry,
Yet trust in Him, our hearts reply.
For every tear, a lesson learned,
In faith's embrace, our souls returned.

From broken paths, He leads us home,
With guiding light, no longer roam.
Each step in grace, a hope reborn,
Through trials fierce, our hearts adorn.

The storms may rage, the night be cold,
Yet in His warmth, we feel consoled.
Restoration comes with love's sweet hand,
In unity, together we stand.

With open arms, He calls us near,
In whispered prayers, we lose our fear.
Through faith, we rise, our burdens shared,
Restored in trust, eternally cared.

So let us walk with hearts so bold,
In every story, His truth unfolds.
To Him we turn, our spirits soar,
In faith's embrace, forevermore.

Sanctified Unity

In sacred bond, our hearts align,
Together strong, our souls entwine.
In kindness spoken, love displayed,
A unity that will not fade.

With open hands, we give our all,
In one accord, we hear the call.
Sanctified by grace divine,
A tapestry of love we find.

Across the miles, our spirits yearn,
In every heart, a flame will burn.
For in His name, we lift our voice,
Embracing peace, we make our choice.

In every step, we seek His way,
With every prayer, our fears allay.
In harmony, our lives reflect,
The sacred bond that we protect.

Together strong, we'll face the storm,
In love we find a holy form.
With faith entwined, no distance wide,
In sanctified unity, we bide.

The Altar of Our Hearts

Upon the altar of the soul,
We gather dreams, we make ourselves whole.
With whispered prayers and hopes held tight,
We seek the dawn, we seek the light.

In silence deep, our hearts converse,
In every trial, a sacred verse.
With gratitude, our essence flows,
As mercy's grace within us grows.

Each tear a gem, each joy a song,
On this altar, we all belong.
In fellowship, our spirits rise,
Reflected love in heavenly skies.

Through every shadow, every doubt,
We find His strength, we find the route.
The altar stands, forever true,
In God's embrace, we are made new.

So let us gather, hand in hand,
In holy love, together we stand.
The altar of our hearts, so pure,
In faith and trust, we shall endure.

Hands Held in Prayer

With hands held high, we draw near,
In silent whispers, we cast out fear.
Together we seek, together we find,
A holy bond in the ties that bind.

In every heartbeat, a prayer ascends,
To love unending, our spirit lends.
With eyes closed tight, our hearts laid bare,
We find our solace, free from despair.

Upon the altar, our burdens shared,
In unity, our hearts are bared.
The power of prayer, a sacred force,
Guiding us gently on the right course.

Through trials faced and tears we shed,
In faithful moments, we forge ahead.
With hands held firm in love's embrace,
We find our hope in His warm grace.

So side by side, we journey forth,
In faith combined, we measure worth.
With hands held high in trust and care,
We walk together, hearts in prayer.

The Bridge of Empathy's Song

In silence we gather, hearts intertwined,
Bridges of care, in the light we find.
Voices of sorrow, whispers of grace,
Empathy builds, a sacred space.

With every heartbeat, rhythms collide,
In the tapestry woven, we rise side by side.
Hands stretched out wide, we share the load,
Together as one, we walk this road.

Through valleys of anguish, joy shall bloom,
Compassion ignites, dispelling the gloom.
Connected in spirit, we journey as kin,
With faith in our hearts, together we win.

Emblems of Trust and Renewal

In the garden of hope, seeds are sown,
Trust is the soil in which love has grown.
Bound by our promise, pure and clear,
With each passing moment, we draw near.

Through trials and storms, we hold the light,
In the darkest of times, we shine so bright.
Emblems of faith carried through the years,
In laughter and love, we face the tears.

Renewal awaits in the dawn's embrace,
In the warmth of our bond, we find our place.
Together we'll rise, a chorus of cheer,
With courage beside us, we conquer fear.

Illuminated by Our Common Struggles

In shadows we wander, seeking the spark,
For in our struggles, we light up the dark.
Shared burdens unite us, hearts intertwined,
Illuminated paths, together we find.

With every trial that shapes our soul,
In the hearts of others, we become whole.
Stories of struggle echo in time,
Uniting our voices, a powerful rhyme.

Together we rise, from ashes we grow,
In the well of our trials, resilience flows.
Bound by compassion, we climb every wall,
In solidarity's grace, we hear the call.

The Sacred Ground of Shared Stories

Upon sacred ground, we gather as one,
With stories to tell, our journeys begun.
Woven together, our hearts open wide,
In the tapestry of life, we will abide.

Each voice a treasure, each tale a thread,
In the chronicles shared, no words left unsaid.
Through laughter and tears, we honor each tale,
In the garden of memories, we shall prevail.

In the bonds of our stories, love shall take flight,
Illuminated pathways, guiding our sight.
Together in spirit, we nurture the flame,
On this sacred ground, we're never the same.

The Light Beckons Beyond the Shadows

In twilight whispers, hope ignites,
A beacon shines, dispelling nights.
With every breath, the spirit wakes,
To dance in light, the soul awakes.

Through valleys deep, where shadows creep,
The light, a promise, soft yet deep.
Its warmth surrounds, a gentle grace,
In every heart, we find our place.

The stars align, the heavens call,
In unity, we stand, we fall.
Together joined, we rise again,
In faith, we break the chains of pain.

So let us walk, hand in hand,
With love as guide, we take our stand.
For though the night may dim our sight,
The dawn will come, a gift of light.

Awake, arise, behold the way,
The light beckons, it's here to stay.
In every heart, a truth resides,
The light of love forever guides.

Harvesting Joy from Wounded Ground

From broken soil, new seeds are sown,
In shadows cast, our strength is grown.
In pain's embrace, the heart does learn,
A lighter spirit, hope must burn.

The raindrops fall, a cleansing grace,
In every tear, a sacred space.
To cultivate what life can yield,
From wounded grounds, our soul is healed.

Together we toil, hands intertwined,
In love's embrace, our hearts aligned.
Through trials faced, we stand as one,
In joy we rise, under the sun.

The colors bloom where hearts have bled,
In every sorrow, joy is fed.
With faith, we gather, hearts anew,
A tapestry of love shines through.

So let us share this fruitful ground,
In unity, our voices sound.
From wounded earth, we reap our share,
With open hearts, we find our prayer.

The Path of Kindred Hearts

Two souls entwined upon the way,
With every step, their spirits play.
In sacred whispers, dreams unfold,
A friendship forged in love so bold.

Through storms and trials, hand in hand,
Together faced, together stand.
In laughter shared, in sorrow's tears,
A bond that deepens through the years.

Kindred hearts, a radiant light,
Guiding each other through the night.
With grace, we walk on paths unknown,
In unity, we find our home.

In visions bright, our dreams entwine,
With faith we journey, hearts align.
For every voice that joins the song,
In harmony, we all belong.

So let us tread this sacred ground,
With kindness shared, our love profound.
In every heartbeat, let us see,
The path of kindred hearts sets free.

Voices Rising in Solace

In stillness found, our voices rise,
A gentle whisper under skies.
In shared embrace, the heart's refrain,
A soothing balm for every pain.

Through shadows cast, the light breaks through,
In every word, a truth rings true.
With every breath, we seek the kind,
In solace found, our souls aligned.

For hearts united cannot break,
In every struggle, love we make.
With open arms, we gather near,
Our voices join, we cast out fear.

In moments shared, the burdens fade,
In harmony, our hearts are laid.
Together strong, we rise and soar,
In love's embrace, we are much more.

So let us sing, with voices clear,
For in our song, the world may hear.
In every note, a sacred taste,
Of love and light, no time to waste.

Mending the Fractured with Compassion

In shadows deep, our hearts do ache,
With hands held high, we mend, not break.
A gentle touch, a whispered prayer,
Together we rise, our burdens share.

From fractured souls, we weave anew,
Compassion's light, in every hue.
In healing's glow, let kindness flow,
With open arms, love's seeds we sow.

We find our strength in every tear,
Uniting hearts, casting out fear.
As we walk forth, side by side,
In compassion's grace, we now abide.

Forgiving past, embracing now,
In every moment, we take a vow.
To mend the world, one heart at a time,
In love's grand dance, we hear the rhyme.

So let us gather, hand in hand,
Mending the fractured across the land.
With compassion's balm, may we ignite,
A world transformed, united in light.

Ascending Through Collective Grace

In unity's fold, we rise in prayer,
Voices lifted, spirits laid bare.
Each heart a note in the sacred song,
Together we stand, where we belong.

Through trials faced, our faith invokes,
A tapestry woven from countless hopes.
With every step, on sacred ground,
In collective grace, our strength is found.

Let love's gentle hand guide us near,
As we ascend, casting away fear.
Each soul a spark, a flame divine,
In shared ascent, our hearts align.

We rise like dawn, breaking the night,
In harmony's glow, we find our light.
Together we soar, on wings of peace,
In collective grace, our burdens cease.

For every struggle, a lesson learned,
Through shared compassion, our spirits burned.
Ascending high, our vision clear,
In love's embrace, forever near.

The Embrace of Anointed Togetherness

In tender whispers, our souls unite,
Anointed warmth in the fading light.
We gather close, in sacred space,
Finding solace in love's embrace.

Each story told, a sacred thread,
In trust and faith, our spirits spread.
Through trials faced, we walk as one,
In togetherness, our work begun.

The heart's soft glow, in darkness shines,
In each embrace, the divine aligns.
Through storms we soar, in every storm,
In unity's grace, our souls transform.

We seek the truth in every face,
In love's reflection, find our place.
With every touch, a blessing shared,
In togetherness, our hearts are bared.

Let us be vessels of peace and light,
In anointed moments, igniting the night.
Through every challenge, we shall find,
In love's embrace, we are entwined.

In the Circle of Renewal

In sacred circles, we gather here,
With open hearts, we cast aside fear.
Each voice a ripple in the serene,
In renewal's light, we breathe, we dream.

The earth beneath, a mother's grace,
In every creature, a holy trace.
We tread with care, on paths divine,
In the circle's fold, our spirits shine.

With hands united, we lift in song,
In every heartbeat, we all belong.
To celebrate life, through joy and pain,
In renewal's cycle, we rise again.

As seasons change, so do we grow,
In love's embrace, we learn to flow.
Each moment sacred, each breath a song,
Together in grace, where we belong.

So let us gather, as one, today,
In the circle of renewal, come what may.
With hearts entwined, may our spirits soar,
In love's embrace, forevermore.

Sacred Bonds

In the quietude of prayer, we find,
Hearts entwined, spirits aligned,
Whispers of faith, a gentle breeze,
Binding souls with sacred ease.

Together we walk on this hallowed ground,
Love and grace in each moment found,
In unity, our voices soar,
Echoing blessings forevermore.

Through trials faced, we stand as one,
Guided by light, our journey begun,
With every step, we grow in trust,
In sacred bonds, we rise from dust.

The tapestry of life, we weave,
In each thread, a promise we believe,
With hands held high, we lift and share,
In love's embrace, find solace there.

With every prayer, our spirits rise,
In the dance of hope, beneath the skies,
Together we sing, in praises loud,
In these sacred bonds, we are endowed.

A Chorus of Redemption

In shadows deep, we search for grace,
A chorus of souls, one sacred space,
With voices raised, in harmony clear,
We gather strength to conquer fear.

From the depths of sorrow, we ascend,
Finding solace in love that will mend,
Each note a promise, each word a balm,
In the heart's embrace, we find our calm.

We sing of mercy, of paths to light,
Redemption's song ignites the night,
With every heartbeat, we are reborn,
In the warmth of Spirit, we're never torn.

With hands together, we forge a bond,
In faith's embrace, our hearts respond,
Through valleys low, and mountains high,
Our chorus rises, a sacred sigh.

A symphony of hope, we play,
Guided by truth, we find our way,
Together we shine, a beacon bright,
In this chorus of love, we take flight.

Risen from the Ashes

In the embers of night, the soul ignites,
From the ashes, it soars to new heights,
With every trial, a lesson learned,
In the fire of struggle, our spirits burned.

Through tears and pain, a seed was sown,
In darkness deep, our truth was shown,
With mighty wings, we rise anew,
Out of the ashes, our spirits grew.

The past, a shadow, but not our chain,
In the light of dawn, we break the pain,
With faith our guide, we step ahead,
In the comfort of hope, we're gently led.

Grounded in love, we flourish bright,
Each breath a testament to the fight,
Together we stand, hearts intertwined,
In every moment, our strength defined.

From sore beginnings, we forge our fate,
In sacred circles, we celebrate,
With eyes wide open, we greet each day,
Risen from ashes, we find our way.

Mosaic of Hope

In fragments scattered, we come together,
A mosaic of hearts, bound like tether,
Each piece a story, each hue a dream,
In the light of grace, we all redeem.

Through trials faced, we learn to stand,
With open hearts, united hand in hand,
In diversity, our colors blend,
Painting a picture that will not end.

Hope is the thread that weaves us tight,
In moments of darkness, it shines so bright,
With every heartbeat, we celebrate,
In this tapestry, love conquers fate.

With each sunrise, the promise renews,
In the sacred dance, we share our views,
Together we rise, as one we sing,
In the mosaic of life, the joy we bring.

In every challenge, we find the grace,
Each piece a blessing, a sacred space,
In the garden of faith, we plant our seeds,
Mosaic of hope, fulfilling our needs.

The Embrace of Spirited Companionship

In the sanctuary of souls we meet,
Walking paths where love is sweet.
With whispers soft as morning light,
We gather strength, dispelling night.

Hand in hand, we share our fears,
Washing wounds with gentle tears.
Each heart's song, a sacred thread,
Weaving hope where once was dread.

In laughter's arms, we find our place,
In silence, feel the warm embrace.
Together, we are never lost,
In unity, we bear our cross.

Through trials storm, our spirits rise,
With faith that reaches to the skies.
No burden too heavy to uphold,
Together, stories yet untold.

So let us walk this holy ground,
In every heartbeat, love is found.
In every glance, a fiery spark,
Illuminating paths through dark.

Stars Aligned in Collective Healing

In the night where shadows play,
The stars align to light our way.
With open hearts, we share our pain,
Transforming losses into gain.

As rivers flow and branches bend,
We seek the truth that sets the trend.
In unity, our spirits mend,
Finding hope in every friend.

Every tear that falls is grace,
Washing sorrow with love's embrace.
In the cycle of the moon,
We find our healing coming soon.

Voices rise, a sacred hymn,
Lifted high, we sing within.
In every note, a shared release,
In harmony, we find our peace.

Collective dreams begin to soar,
Igniting hearts to seek for more.
With every pulse, a chance to shine,
Together, love will intertwine.

Echoes of Forgiveness in the Void

In the silence where echoes dwell,
We find the stories we must tell.
Forgiveness blooms like springtime's grace,
Filling the shadows with its embrace.

As gentle winds whisper our name,
Releasing burdens, quenching blame.
With every step, we turn the page,
Finding light in grief's sad wage.

In the mirror of souls, we see,
The power of love to set us free.
In every heart, a sacred vow,
To heal the wounds, to lift the now.

Let the past not hold us king,
In our hearts, new choices spring.
With open arms, we face the dawn,
In forgiveness, we are reborn.

Together, we will rise above,
Embracing all with endless love.
In the void, a voice will sing,
Of hope and peace the future brings.

The Gentle Rhythm of Unity's Heart

As waves caress the sandy shore,
We find a rhythm, evermore.
In every heartbeat, a perfect tune,
Guiding us beneath the moon.

With hands united, we draw near,
Sharing dreams, dispelling fear.
In harmony, our spirits blend,
Creating peace that has no end.

In sacred circles, we embrace,
Every laugh, a sacred place.
In each sigh, a promise made,
In unity, our fears will fade.

Let the tempo soar and rise,
With every step, we touch the skies.
Together, we will dance and sway,
In love's embrace, we find our way.

So let us listen to the sound,
Of unity, forever bound.
With gentle hearts, we play our part,
In the rhythm of life's great heart.

The Ties That Renew

In the silence of the dawn, we convene,
Hearts entwined, spirits keen.
Grace flows like a gentle stream,
Binding us in a sacred dream.

Beneath the shadows of ancient trees,
We find solace in whispered pleas.
Hands uplifted, eyes to the skies,
In this moment, love never dies.

Together we weave a tapestry bright,
Threads of hope in the soft twilight.
Through trials faced, we come to know,
The ties that bind, they strengthen and grow.

With each step taken on this shared way,
We remember love's gentle sway.
In faith's embrace, we are renewed,
Bound forever, our hearts imbued.

And as the night falls, we gather near,
With voices united in praise, sincere.
For in this communion of souls so true,
We celebrate the ties that renew.

A Pilgrimage of Grace

With each dawn, we rise to seek,
A path where light and love speak.
Through valleys low and mountains high,
In every heart, a longing sigh.

A pilgrimage on sacred ground,
In the stillness, truth is found.
We walk in faith, hand in hand,
With hope, the light we understand.

Every step whispers a prayer,
In the messengers' gentle care.
To the horizon, our eyes are cast,
For in the journey, shadows pass.

In trials faced, we find our strength,
Love's embrace, a blessed length.
As we venture, spirits soar,
In grace, we seek, forevermore.

At the end, a banquet awaits,
Sharing joy beyond the gates.
Together, we sing a song of grace,
A pilgrimage of love in this sacred space.

In the Footsteps of Belief

In the footsteps of those who've gone,
We find our way, our spirits drawn.
Through tales of old, they guide our path,
In their wisdom, we escape wrath.

With every breath, we seek the light,
In darkness, they shine ever bright.
Their legacy, a sacred flame,
In our hearts, we honor their name.

We tread softly on this sacred land,
In unity, together we stand.
At the edge of doubt, faith ignites,
Guided by love through countless nights.

In trials faced, we learn and grow,
A tapestry of belief we sew.
Through storms of life, we shall prevail,
In the footsteps of belief, we sail.

And as we journey, hand in hand,
In love's embrace, we understand.
There's strength in our shared faith's call,
In the footsteps of belief, we stand tall.

Harmony in Prayer

In whispers soft, our hearts align,
In harmony, souls intertwine.
Each prayer rises, a fragrant plea,
Uniting us in sacred decree.

With hands uplifted to the skies,
In silence deep, the spirit flies.
Every murmur, a gentle grace,
In this stillness, we find our place.

Through trials shared, we draw near,
In love's embrace, we cast out fear.
For every tear, a flower blooms,
In harmony, the heart resumes.

Voices lift in sweet refrain,
In sacred spaces, we remain.
Each thought a light, each hope a glow,
In harmony, we learn and grow.

And as the evening shadows creep,
In prayerful hope, our dreams we keep.
Together, we shall softly sway,
In the rhythm of love, harmony in prayer.

United in Sacred Reverie

In the stillness of prayer, we unite,
Hearts lifted high, reaching for the light.
Voices mingle in a sacred embrace,
Together we find our spiritual place.

With every whisper, a promise we weave,
In faith and in love, we truly believe.
Gathered in harmony, souls intertwined,
Boundless devotion, our hearts aligned.

Chasing shadows, we seek the divine,
Each step we take, a celestial sign.
Embracing the silence, we hear the call,
In this sacred space, we surrender all.

Through trials and storms, we stand as one,
In the tapestry of life, we are spun.
With hands held gently, we share our plight,
In sacred reverie, we shine so bright.

Within this bond, there's strength to rise,
Lifting each other toward the skies.
In unity's song, we find our way,
United in sacred, we cherish the sway.

The Kinship of Kindness

In gentle hearts, love's whispers reside,
A kinship of kindness, our true guide.
With every smile, a bridge we create,
Together we nurture, together we wait.

The world can be harsh, but we are the light,
Guiding the weary through the dark night.
In acts of compassion, we find our grace,
The kinship of kindness, our sacred space.

Every hand extended, a blessing so pure,
In simple gestures, our spirits endure.
We lift up the fallen, we carry the load,
In the warmth of our hearts, love's seed is sowed.

Through laughter and tears, our spirits entwine,
In kindness, we flourish, like fruit on the vine.
In this holy circle, we've come to believe,
That the kinship of kindness, we each can conceive.

As our paths converge in life's fleeting dance,
In kindness, we flourish, we take the chance.
With each selfless act, the world we embrace,
In love's warm embrace, we find our place.

Nurtured by Light

In the dawn's warm glow, our spirits awake,
Nurtured by light, the path we take.
With hope in our hearts, we rise to greet,
The blessings of life, in the quiet retreat.

Through trials faced, we reclaim our sight,
In the darkest moments, we search for the light.
With faith as our anchor, we journey along,
Nurtured by light, we find where we belong.

Every step forward, a beacon so bright,
Guiding our way through the long, starry night.
In silence and stillness, our souls find their might,
In the tender embrace of love's pure light.

With wisdom that grows, we gather and share,
In the warmth of the sun, there's kindness laid bare.
Nurtured by light, we sow seeds of grace,
Illuminated hearts in our sacred space.

As the seasons change, we learn and we grow,
In gratitude's song, our spirits will flow.
In unity's journey, our souls take flight,
Forever we're grateful, nurtured by light.

The Flame of Communion

In the circle of life, a flame softly glows,
The flame of communion, where love truly flows.
With hearts intertwined, we gather around,
In this sacred moment, our souls are unbound.

Through whispers of prayer, we ignite the spark,
In the quiet of night, we light up the dark.
Each voice a melody, in harmony's tune,
The flame of communion, like petals in bloom.

With offerings shared, we kindle the fire,
Bound by the spirit that lifts us higher.
In moments of stillness, we feel the embrace,
As the flame of communion ignites our grace.

In laughter and tears, the flame ever bright,
Guiding our journey, a beacon of light.
Through trials and triumphs, we hold tight the flame,
In the heart of communion, we honor the name.

As we gather together, the circle expands,
In the warmth of our love, we join hand in hand.
The flame of communion forever will last,
In unity's embrace, we honor the past.

The Poetry of Shared Blessings

In the dawn of grace we meet,
Hands together, hearts beat.
Voices mingle in the air,
Lifted prayers, a sacred care.

Each blessing shared, a radiant thread,
Connecting souls where love is spread.
In every smile a light shines through,
A gift of peace in all we do.

Gathered round this hallowed space,
Divine mercy, our embrace.
In the quiet, faith ignites,
Illuminating darkest nights.

With gratitude, our hearts take flight,
Finding strength in shared delight.
Together we rise, never apart,
United in the realm of heart.

So let us weave this tapestry,
Of kindness, hope, and harmony.
A symphony of love we sing,
In the joy that sharing brings.

Blossoms of Unity in the Spirit's Garden

In the garden where we stand,
Blooming petals, hand in hand.
Colors vibrant, nature's art,
Reflections of the joyful heart.

Each flower whispers tales of grace,
In unity, we find our place.
Sunlight paints the path we tread,
With faith as roots, our spirits spread.

Together, let compassion grow,
Nurtured by the love we sow.
In every bloom, His light be found,
A sacred bond that knows no bound.

As we gather, souls align,
In this sacred space, divine.
Each petal holds a story true,
Of shared blessings, me and you.

In the spirit's garden bright,
We flourish under God's sweet light.
Let hearts unite, a chorus swell,
In harmony, all shall dwell.

The Gathering of Sacred Hearts

In this circle of sacred grace,
We gather, each soul, a trace.
With open hearts and minds so free,
Together bound in unity.

Through trials faced and joys embraced,
The love of God is interlaced.
In every tear and laughter shared,
A testament of how we cared.

Each sacred heart, a beacon bright,
Shining hope in darkest night.
With gentle hands, we lift and mend,
In this sacred place, we blend.

Let kindness weave its tender thread,
In every word that's gently said.
As brothers, sisters, we do rise,
Together painting endless skies.

In the gathering, we find our soul,
A sacred mission, a common goal.
In love's embrace, our spirits soar,
Together as one, forevermore.

Whispers in the Sanctuary

In the stillness, whispers flow,
Echoes of the heart's great show.
In this sanctuary's warm embrace,
We find our refuge, God's own grace.

Softly spoken, prayers take flight,
Guided by the holy light.
Every word, a sacred plea,
Connecting us eternally.

In the quiet, wisdom speaks,
In the silence, spirit seeks.
Here we gather, souls align,
In harmony, the Divine.

With every breath, we feel the peace,
In each moment, blessings increase.
United hearts, a tapestry,
Woven close in unity.

So let us treasure this time anew,
In the sanctuary, me and you.
With whispers soft, our voices blend,
In the love of God, we transcend.

Wings of Hope

In shadows deep, where fears reside,
A whisper calls, a gentle guide.
With wings of hope, we rise and soar,
To brighter paths, forevermore.

Through trials faced, we stand as one,
In faith's embrace, our race begun.
The light will break, the dawn will gleam,
In unity, we chase the dream.

When storms may rage, and tempests howl,
We lift each other, hearts avow.
With trust as fuel, we journey on,
For in this bond, our souls be drawn.

Each tear we shed, a sacred rite,
A symbol of our shared plight.
With every step, a prayer unfolds,
In love's embrace, our hope enfolds.

So let us rise, with spirits high,
With wings of hope, we touch the sky.
Together strong, we'll face the night,
In faith and love, we find the light.

The Covenant of Togetherness

In community's heart, we find our way,
A covenant made, come what may.
Hand in hand, we forge a bond,
In love and grace, we all respond.

Through joys and trials, our spirits blend,
In whispered prayers, our voices send.
Together we'll stand, steadfast and true,
In every moment, I'll be with you.

The sacred ties that bind us tight,
Illuminate paths in darkest night.
No distance great, nor stormy sea,
Can sever the love that flows so free.

With hearts entwined, we laugh and cry,
We build our dreams, with hope we fly.
In every challenge, hand in hand,
We honor the vows that we have planned.

So raise your voice, let praises swell,
For in togetherness, all is well.
In unity strong, we rise and sing,
The covenant of love, our eternal spring.

Illuminated by Forgiveness

In quiet whispers, burdens release,
Forgiveness blooms, granting peace.
With open hearts and minds that mend,
We find our way, we start to blend.

The past may haunt, yet we let go,
In forgiveness' light, our spirits grow.
Each act of grace, a step we take,
To heal the wounds, for love's sweet sake.

Embrace the shadows that once held tight,
Transforming darkness into light.
With every word of kindness spoken,
A bridge is built, no longer broken.

Forgiveness flows like rivers wide,
Washing away the pain and pride.
In this sacred act, we find our way,
Guided by love, come what may.

So let us walk this path anew,
Illuminated by the truth we knew.
In forgiveness' grace, we rise and stand,
Together in peace, hand in hand.

Sacred Threads of Connection

In every soul, a thread is spun,
Connecting hearts, we are all one.
Through laughter's joy and sorrow's veil,
The sacred bonds shall never fail.

With open arms, we weave our fate,
Embracing all, we cultivate.
In every smile, in every tear,
The sacred threads draw us near.

Through life's tapestry, rich and vast,
Our shared experiences bind us fast.
With love as thread, we stitch and sew,
Creating beauty from what we know.

In every encounter, the divine appears,
A reflection of hopes, joys, and fears.
Each moment shared, a precious gift,
In every connection, our spirits lift.

So let us honor these threads we share,
In unity, we breathe the air.
For in this world, so vast and wide,
The sacred threads connect our stride.

The River of Renewal

In the heart of the valley, flows pure and clear,
A river of renewal, washing away fear.
It whispers of hope, in every soft sway,
Guiding the lost, towards a brighter day.

With waters that spark, life anew does rise,
Miraculously quenched, beneath the vast skies.
It carries our burdens, each sorrowful tear,
All troubles dissolve, in the current so dear.

The rocks stand as witnesses, to stories untold,
Of faith and of struggle, of new and of old.
Embracing each heartbeat, as secrets unwind,
The river flows gently, uniting mankind.

In shadows of trees that bend low to the stream,
We find in our stillness, a moment to dream.
The river, our shepherd, guides us to grace,
In every reflection, we witness His face.

Under One Blessed Sky

Beneath the vast heavens, our spirits take flight,
Together in worship, we gather, unite.
The stars are our candles, lit in the night,
Each twinkling a promise, of love and of light.

In the stillness of dawn, we raise up our voice,
A chorus of hope, in one heart, rejoice.
The sun breaks the silence, colors the day,
Under one blessed sky, we kneel, and we pray.

Each cloud holds our dreams, each breeze brings a song,
Together we journey, united and strong.
With faith as our anchor, we shall not be swayed,
For under this heaven, His love won't soon fade.

In moments of trial, we stand hand in hand,
With grace as our guide, we will always withstand.
The warmth of His presence, our shadows outshine,
Under one blessed sky, His promise we find.

As sunset paints gold, the horizon aglow,
We gather in spirit, no bonds we outgrow.
With hearts interwoven, we make our plea,
Under one blessed sky, forever we'll be.

Walking on Sacred Ground

With every soft step, in the whispering grove,
I tread on the path, where the ancients rove.
Each stone tells a story, of prayers and of grace,
In walking on sacred ground, I find my place.

Surrounded by nature, His presence is felt,
In the rustle of leaves, my heart starts to melt.
The fragrance of blossoms, fills air with delight,
As I wander in wonder, from day into night.

In the hush of the forest, I hear the divine,
A calling that leads, with a whispering sign.
The beauty of creation, reflects His plan,
Walking on sacred ground, I know I am man.

Each footprint is marked, by love's gentle hand,
In this hallowed space, together we stand.
With faith as our compass, and hope as our guide,
On sacred ground walking, in Him we confide.

As twilight descends, I give thanks and I pray,
For the peace that surrounds me, in every way.
In each moment of silence, my spirit is found,
In journeying onward, on sacred ground.

Consolation in Faith's Embrace

In the quiet of night, when shadows creep near,
I find my solace, in faith without fear.
With each whispered prayer, I surrender my doubt,
In the warmth of His love, I feel peace throughout.

Though storms may surround, I will not despair,
For strength in His arms, is a comfort so rare.
In valleys of anguish, where tears tend to flow,
Consolation in faith, is the light that will glow.

With hope as my beacon, I tread the unknown,
In the depths of despair, I'm never alone.
Each heartache I bear, draws me closer within,
Finding strength in the promise, where new life begins.

In moments of silence, His whispers I hear,
With courage I face, what I once held in fear.
Faith's embrace is tender, a refuge to find,
In the tapestry woven, my heart's forever aligned.

So let not the trials, deepen your plight,
For in faith's gentle arms, there's a guiding light.
With every new dawn, I rise up anew,
Consolation in faith, forever I'll pursue.

Stardust of Shared Aspirations

In the night, stars twinkle bright,
Whispers of dreams take their flight.
Each heart beats in harmony's grace,
Guiding us to a sacred place.

Together we weave a tapestry fine,
Threads of hope, with love they entwine.
In unity's glow, we rise above,
Illuminated by faith's pure love.

Winds of change, they softly blow,
In the journey, we learn and grow.
Every prayer a spark divine,
Melding our spirits, your hand in mine.

As stardust falls, we dare to dream,
Reflections of light in the moonbeam.
Each aspiration shared with trust,
A testament forged in the sacred dust.

We stand on the cusp, where hopes entwine,
Together we reach, to the holy shrine.
In the silence, we courageously dare,
To lift our voices in fervent prayer.

Paths of Rising Light

In quiet dawn, the shadows fade,
Hope unfolds, new paths are laid.
With each step, a light bestowed,
Guiding us on this sacred road.

We walk this journey hand in hand,
Faithful hearts, united we stand.
Through valleys deep and mountains high,
Together we sing, our spirits fly.

The sun ascends, casting golden beams,
Illuminating all our dreams.
In the warmth of love's embrace,
We find our truth, our rightful place.

In every shadow, a lesson learned,
In every trial, our spirits burned.
The light within shall ever shine,
Bringing forth the divine design.

As souls converge on this path we roam,
Ever closer to our heavenly home.
With joyful hearts, we take our flight,
On paths illuminated by rising light.

Where Souls Converge

In the quiet of the evening's grace,
Souls gather in this holy space.
Hearts entwined in love's sweet song,
In this embrace, where we belong.

With every whisper, unity swells,
Among the echoes, peace dwells.
The light of hope shines ever clear,
Binding us close, drawing us near.

As we share our stories, pure and true,
In the sacred bond, I see you.
Through trials faced, and joys proclaimed,
In this circle, love is named.

Where souls converge, we rise as one,
Beneath the blessings of the sun.
In the arms of grace, we find release,
With open hearts, we share our peace.

Let us dance in this sacred light,
Together, we shine through the night.
In the sanctuary of each embrace,
We find our strength, our sacred space.

One Voice in Worship

In the stillness, our hearts align,
Voices rising, a sacred sign.
Breath of the Spirit, filling the air,
Together we gather in fervent prayer.

With every note, our souls uplift,
In the chorus, we find love's gift.
Harmony flows through every vein,
Binding us close in joy and pain.

Hands held high, in reverence we stand,
With gratitude, we offer our hands.
In this moment, divinely led,
Hearts united, no words left unsaid.

In the togetherness, we find our might,
Like stars that shimmer in the night.
A single voice in a timeless hymn,
Resounding truth, never dim.

As we worship, our spirits soar,
In one voice, we open the door.
To the infinite grace that binds us tight,
In unity, we bask in the light.

In Search of the Divine Touch

In the silence of the night, we pray,
Yearning for light to guide our way.
Whispers of hope in the stillness dwell,
Longing for a touch, a sacred spell.

Beneath the stars, we cast our hearts,
Seeking the truth where each journey starts.
In the shadows, His mercy shines,
Breaking the chains of earthly confines.

Through trials faced and burdens borne,
In every tear, a promise worn.
With every heartbeat, we seek to find,
The gentle caress of the divine mind.

In every prayer, a voice so clear,
Drawing us close, dispelling fear.
United in faith, our spirits soar,
In search of the touch we all adore.

Let us lift our souls to the sky,
Holding each moment as we sigh.
In every heartbeat, the divine we clutch,
In the sacred embrace, we find our touch.

A Lament for Love and Friendship

In shadows cast by time's cruel hand,
We wander through memories, like grains of sand.
Once bright laughter fills the air,
Now echoes linger, a wistful prayer.

The bonds we forged in youthful glee,
Now drift like leaves from the wise old tree.
A silent ache in every glance,
In moments missed, we mourn our chance.

Together we danced on dreams we spun,
But the threads have frayed, our laughter done.
Yet in my heart, your spirit stays,
A gentle warmth on colder days.

O fragile ties, how they intertwine,
Through joy and sorrow, they brightly shine.
In the quiet of night, I remember well,
The love and friendship, our sacred shell.

But every tear that falls unwinds,
A testament to the love that binds.
So here I stand with open heart,
In memory's embrace, we never part.

The Mosaic of Faith

In every heart, a fragment lies,
A piece of truth beneath the skies.
We gather shards from those before,
Creating beauty, forevermore.

With colors bright, our stories blend,
In unity, the broken mend.
Each tile a prayer, each hue a song,
In the hands of grace, we all belong.

Through valleys deep and mountains high,
With hands outstretched, we learn to fly.
Faith weaves a tapestry of hope,
With every thread, we learn to cope.

In laughter shared, in whispered dreams,
We find the light in faith's soft beams.
Together we stand, though storms may rage,
In the mosaic of love, we turn the page.

For every heart that seeks the dawn,
In the morning light, we all are drawn.
United in faith, our spirits rise,
In every glance, the divine ties.

A Union of Heartstrings

Two souls entwined, a sacred dance,
In the rhythm of time, we take our chance.
With every heartbeat, the bond grows tight,
Guided by love, through day and night.

In the quiet whispers, our secrets lie,
A song of devotion that reaches the sky.
In laughter shared and pain endured,
The union of heartstrings, forever secured.

Through trials faced, together we stand,
With faith and trust, we join hand in hand.
Each moment cherished, each tear embraced,
In the sacred space where love is traced.

Across the winds of fate we glide,
In the whispers of faith, we coincide.
Two hearts, one journey, a radiant light,
In the union of heartstrings, we take flight.

For every heartbeat sings our song,
In the dance of love, we all belong.
Together we weave, in tender grace,
A union of heartstrings, a sweet embrace.

The Resonance of Compassion

In hearts of stone, grace flows like a stream,
A soft embrace, a tender dream.
Love whispers loud in silent halls,
Where kindness rises, and hatred falls.

With open hands, we share our light,
Through darkest paths, we shine so bright.
Each gentle word a healing balm,
A sacred chant, a holy psalm.

We gather close, no soul alone,
In unity, we find our home.
Let mercy guide our every breath,
In love we rise, in hate we cease.

Forgiveness flows like rivers wide,
Together still, with hearts as one.
In resonance, our spirits soar,
With compassion's strength, we shall endure.

For in the end, it's love that stays,
A beacon bright through all our days.
Let us reflect this sacred grace,
In every heart, in every space.

Woven in Praise

In fragrant blooms and soaring skies,
Creation sings, each soul replies.
Threads of beauty, woven tight,
In humble hearts, we find the light.

From mountains high to oceans deep,
Each whispered prayer we gently keep.
In silent woods, the moments cling,
To nature's hymn, our voices sing.

With every dawn, we lift our eyes,
And find our faith in morning's rise.
A tapestry of grace we weave,
In every breath, we do believe.

Through trials faced and shadows cast,
In love's embrace, we hold steadfast.
Each note we share, a sacred sound,
In joy and sorrow, peace is found.

Together bound, in praise we stand,
In every heartbeat, God's own hand.
We celebrate, in joy, we raise,
Our voices high, in woven praise.

The Crystal Waters of Belief

In tranquil pools where spirits flow,
The crystal waters gently glow.
Reflecting truths both deep and clear,
In silent prayer, our hearts draw near.

Each drop a story, pure as light,
A journey long from dark to bright.
With every sip, our souls renew,
In faith's embrace, we rise and grew.

The ripples dance on sacred shores,
An echo of the love that pours.
In every wave, a promise found,
In open hearts, the world resounds.

In stillness, find the strength to trust,
In gentle waters, pure and just.
Beneath the surface, peace resides,
As hope and grace, in us, abides.

Let crystal streams their wisdom share,
In every soul, a spirit rare.
Flow freely forth; let love increase,
In waters pure, we find our peace.

Embracing the Celestial

In starlit nights, our spirits soar,
As dreams take flight, forevermore.
With open arms, we reach the sky,
Where whispers of the angels lie.

In every twinkle, light divine,
Inviting us to realms that shine.
Across the vast and endless space,
We glimpse the love in every place.

Each moment shared beneath the moon,
A hymn of hope, a sacred tune.
With sky above and earth below,
In unity, our faith will grow.

Embrace the wonder of the stars,
Forgiveness found through all our scars.
In cosmic dance, we twirl and spin,
With heavens open, we journey in.

To grasp the celestial truth we seek,
In quiet moments, hear love speak.
We are but threads in Heaven's weave,
In every heartbeat, we believe.

Beneath the Wings of Mercy

In shadows deep, where sorrows lie,
The heart finds peace, through whispered sighs.
Beneath the wings, of solace sweet,
Our weary souls, in love shall meet.

A gentle grace, enfolds us whole,
In divine light, we find our role.
With every breath, a prayer we raise,
In gratitude, we walk our days.

Through trials faced, and burdens borne,
The dawn shall break, a new day's morn.
In mercy's arms, we find our rest,
Through trials passed, we are truly blessed.

In every tear, a lesson sown,
In every joy, His love is shown.
Together, we stand, ever strong,
In sacred trust, we all belong.

So lift your voice, and praise His name,
For in His light, we are the same.
Beneath the wings, forever near,
In mercy's grace, we have no fear.

The Covenant of Kindred Spirits

From hearts entwined, a bond is grew,
In faith we walk, the path is true.
With every step, our spirits soar,
In love and light, we are restored.

Together we share, each joy and tear,
In unity's strength, we conquer fear.
The covenant formed, in sacred trust,
In gentle whispers, we are just.

In trials faced, together we stand,
With open hearts, we join our hands.
For in this life, we find our peace,
In every moment, our joys increase.

Through darkest nights, a guiding star,
Our souls aligned, we've come so far.
In kindness shown, we find our way,
In every heart, a brighter day.

So let us sing, our spirits free,
In harmony, we shall agree.
With love abundant, we find our role,
In kindred spirits, we are whole.

A Chorus of Hope's Resilience

In echoes bright, the voices rise,
A chorus swells, beneath the skies.
With every note, a spirit found,
In hope's embrace, we are unbound.

Through darkest nights, we sing as one,
A melody bright, when all is done.
With every heart, a beat in time,
In harmony, our souls will climb.

Resilient hearts, in trials faced,
In every moment, love is traced.
Together we rise, as shadows flee,
In faith and trust, we will be free.

So let us raise, our voices high,
In joy and peace, beneath the sky.
For in this song, is strength anew,
A chorus born, from me and you.

In every tear, a spark ignites,
In hope's embrace, we find our lights.
So let the world, hear our refrain,
In unity, we shall remain.

Rivers of Compassion Flow

From hearts expressed, like rivers wide,
Compassion flows, with gentle tide.
In every hand, a kindness shared,
In selfless acts, we've truly cared.

A soothing balm, for weary souls,
In every drop, a story holds.
With open hearts, we reach to heal,
In love's embrace, our spirits feel.

Through trials faced, we find our way,
In sunny skies or skies of gray.
As rivers merge, our paths align,
In every life, His love shall shine.

So let us flow, like water pure,
In every heart, our hopes endure.
For in our gifts, we find our worth,
In every act, we bless this earth.

With every tear, a river springs,
In compassion's song, our spirit sings.
Together we stand, as rivers do,
In empathy's tide, we are made new.

Whispers of the Soul's Embrace

In quiet moments, hearts reveal,
A gentle touch, a sacred seal.
The whispers of the soul, they rise,
Embraced beneath the endless skies.

Through trials worn, we seek the light,
In darkness deep, we find our height.
Each prayer a strand, a lifeline cast,
To weave our futures from the past.

Where love abounds, the spirits soar,
Within each heart, the open door.
We gather close, in faith we stand,
With open arms, a steady hand.

A journey shared, in grace we move,
Through storms and trials, we find our groove.
In whispers soft, our hopes align,
Bound by the threads of the divine.

So let us walk, in peace arrayed,
Together strong, our fears allayed.
With souls embraced, in love's sweet flow,
We find our strength, together grow.

Under the Canopy of Grace

Beneath the boughs of gentle trees,
We find a love that sets us free.
In every leaf and rustling sound,
The grace of God, in love abound.

As shadows dance in sunlight's glow,
We learn to trust, to let love flow.
Each moment shared, a sacred bond,
In silence deep, of Him we're fond.

With every prayer, our spirits rise,
In harmony, we hear His ties.
Resilient hearts, our voices blend,
A melody that will not end.

In shared reflections, peace is found,
With faith, our roots grow deep in ground.
Under the sky, we bow in grace,
Embraced within this holy place.

So let us walk, hand in hand with light,
Through every loss, we will ignite.
In unity, our souls will trace,
The journey home, our paths interlace.

Threads of Light in Unity

In sacred circles, hearts entwined,
Threads of light, together lined.
We weave our hopes, a tapestry,
Of faith and love, our legacy.

Each voice a note in harmony,
A chorus strong, a symphony.
With every prayer, our hearts ignite,
In shared belief, we find the light.

Through trials faced, we stand as one,
In moments dark, we find the sun.
With open hearts, we share our way,
In light's embrace, we'll always stay.

So let us shout, our praises clear,
In unity, we hold what's dear.
Each thread we spin, a bond we weave,
In love's embrace, we all believe.

Together strong, our spirits rise,
With every step beneath the skies.
In faith's embrace, we find our place,
Threads of light, in unity, grace.

Sanctuary of Shared Sorrows

In sacred space where hearts unfold,
We gather close, our stories told.
With every tear, a bond we form,
In sorrow's weight, we find the warm.

Through every trial, hand in hand,
We lift each other, here we stand.
Each whispered prayer, a gentle balm,
In shared sorrow, we find the calm.

The burdens light, when shared with grace,
In every heart, a holy place.
Through pain endured, we break the chains,
In unity, our spirit reigns.

So let the walls of fear fall down,
In love's embrace, we wear the crown.
In this sanctuary, we'll abide,
With open hearts, and love as guide.

Together we rise, in faith we trust,
With every step, it's love we must.
In shared sorrows, we find our way,
A brighter dawn, a hopeful day.

United in Sacred Light

In shadows deep, we seek your face,
With open hearts, we find our place.
Together, Lord, we share this grace,
In sacred light, we hold your trace.

With every step, we walk as one,
In unity, your will be done.
From every tribe, your love is spun,
In harmony, we rise like sun.

Our voices lifted, songs of praise,
In joyful hearts, your glory stays.
With faith ignited, we embrace,
In sacred light, we find our ways.

Through trials faced, we stand so strong,
In every heart, a holy song.
With love's embrace, where we belong,
In sacred light, we won't go wrong.

Together bound, in faith's delight,
We shine as stars, through darkest night.
With every prayer, our souls take flight,
In your embrace, we find our sight.

The Covenant of Compassion

In humble hearts, we pledge our care,
With open hands, we strive to share.
Through joy and pain, we learn to bear,
In love's embrace, our burdens rare.

Your voice calls out, in gentle tones,
To build a world where love atones.
From every wound, your mercy loans,
In compassion's arms, our hope is sown.

With every tear, a promise made,
In silence deep, your light won't fade.
Together strong, we shall not trade,
For kindness' grace is never weighed.

In every act, your spirit shines,
Through giving hearts, your love aligns.
In every soul, a spark divine,
In compassion's name, our fates combine.

With hands entwined, we walk this road,
In every heart, your love bestowed.
With every deed, our faith is sowed,
In covenant, our spirits glowed.

Bound by Grace

In valleys low, you lift us high,
With gentle touch, you dry our eye.
Through every storm, we learn to fly,
In boundless grace, we will not die.

Your love envelops, strong and warm,
In all we face, you are the balm.
With every heartbeat, still we charm,
In whispered hope, we find our calm.

Together we stand, through dark and light,
In unity, we choose what's right.
With faith as guide, our spirits bright,
In bound by grace, we share the fight.

In every challenge, strength is found,
Through every trial, we stand our ground.
With every voice, your love resounds,
In grace, our hearts and lives are crowned.

With every step, we walk in trust,
In every moment, rise we must.
In grace's bond, our hearts combust,
And in your love, we place our trust.

Embrace of the Divine

In silence deep, your presence glows,
In every breath, your love bestows.
With open arms, the spirit flows,
In embrace divine, our faith grows.

Through trials faced, you hold us near,
In every sorrow, calm our fear.
With gentle whispers, you are clear,
In love's embrace, we persevere.

With hearts attuned, we seek your face,
In every action, show your grace.
Through joy and pain, we find our place,
In sacred love, our souls interlace.

Through every path, your light we trace,
In every shadow, find your space.
With faith united, we embrace,
In your warm light, we leave a trace.

Together bound, we seek your way,
In every moment, night or day.
With grateful hearts, our voices sway,
In embrace divine, we choose to stay.

Whirlwinds of Love and Resilience

In the tempest, hope takes flight,
Love's embrace, our guiding light.
Through the storms, we stand so tall,
Together, we shall never fall.

When shadows loom and hearts grow cold,
Resilience rises, brave and bold.
With every whisper, hearts entwine,
Bound by faith, a love divine.

In trials faced, we find our grace,
An infinite bond, a warm embrace.
With open arms, we break the chains,
In unity, joy remains.

As whirlwinds howl, we hold our ground,
In sacred circles, strength is found.
Through myriad storms and darkest night,
Love's resilience will always ignite.

With every struggle, courage blooms,
In valleys deep, through shadows' glooms.
Together we rise, fierce and free,
In the whirlwind's dance, we shall be.

Rebuilding Ruins with Words of Faith

In shattered places, hope resides,
With words of faith, our hearts are tied.
Through broken stones, we weave a prayer,
A tapestry of love laid bare.

Each voice a beacon, bright and true,
In silence, dreams are born anew.
With gentle strength, we lift the veil,
Rebuilding ruins where love prevails.

Through trials faced and burdens shared,
In whispered faith, we are prepared.
With hands united, we pave the way,
For brighter morns to greet the day.

As faith ignites, our spirits soar,
Resilience blooms from every core.
Through cracks of sorrow, flowers grow,
In sacred unity, we sow.

With open hearts, we mend the seams,
In every word, a dream redeems.
Through faith and love, we rise again,
In the ruins, hope shall reign.

The Oasis of Understanding Awaits

In the desert of doubt, we seek a guide,
An oasis of grace where hearts confide.
With open minds, we share our fears,
In understanding's light, we shed our tears.

Through every story, wisdom flows,
A sanctuary where true love grows.
With gentle words, we heal the pain,
In unity, our spirits gain.

As rivers meet, the soul's embrace,
In harmony's tune, we find our place.
With listening ears, we tread the path,
In kindness, we quell the aftermath.

In the oasis, trust takes root,
With every footstep, we stand astute.
Through seasons' change, we hold the space,
In understanding, we find our grace.

As mirage fades, the truth shines bright,
In shared compassion, we ignite.
Together we journey, hand in hand,
To the oasis, where hearts expand.

In the Spirit of Compassionate Kinship

In the spirit of kinship, hearts align,
Compassionate whispers, a sacred sign.
With arms wide open, we greet the day,
In love's embrace, we find our way.

As kindred souls, we walk this path,
In unity's grace, we share the laugh.
Through trials faced, together we rise,
In every struggle, our spirit flies.

With gentle courage, we lift each other,
In the warmth of love, we find a mother.
Through storms we weather, side by side,
In truth and kindness, we shall abide.

As hearts entwined in sacred trust,
In every action, we find the just.
Through heartfelt gestures, our spirits blend,
In the spirit of kinship, there's no end.

In moments shared, we make a stand,
In love's embrace, we understand.
Forever bound in love's sweet refrain,
In compassionate kinship, we remain.

Communion of Hearts

In silence we gather, hands entwined,
Each heart beats a hymn, so divine.
Whispers of faith in the cool night air,
Our spirits unite in a moment so rare.

We share in the bounty of love so clear,
In the glow of the moon, we cast off our fear.
Each prayer like a river, flows smooth and wide,
Together in purpose, we walk side by side.

With every soft smile, a promise we make,
To cherish each other, our bond will not break.
In the warmth of this circle, no soul stands apart,
A sanctuary built in the depth of each heart.

Through trials and tribulations, we rise,
Guided by faith and the light in our eyes.
In this sacred moment, we find our way home,
In the communion of hearts, forever we roam.

As dawn gently comes, with a blush in the sky,
We leave with the wisdom that love will not die.
Each heart we've connected, a thread in the weave,
In the tapestry of faith, we learn to believe.

Together in the Light of Truth

In the still of the morn, we find our way,
Through shadows of doubt, we choose to stay.
With voices like candles, we sing our plea,
In unity formed, from chains we are free.

The truth guides our spirits, a beacon so bright,
Illuminating pathways that once lost their light.
Each step that we take, with purpose we tread,
Together we journey, where angels have led.

In the warmth of your gaze, I find solace deep,
A promise of hope that the heavens keep.
Through storm and through trial, we stand hand in hand,
In the arms of the light, we forever will stand.

With faith as our armor, love as our sword,
We rise in the knowledge, our spirits restored.
Nameless and timeless, we dwell ever near,
Together in truth, we conquer our fear.

As night gently falls, with stars shining bright,
We gather like moths, drawn to the light.
In the stillness we whisper, our hearts interlace,
Together in the truth, we find our true place.

Under Heaven's Watchful Eye

In the arms of the evening, we pause and reflect,
Under heaven's gaze, we feel its protect.
Each star a reminder of love that surrounds,
In solace we find the grace that abounds.

In the hush of the twilight, our worries subside,
With whispers of hope, we open wide.
The world may be burdensome, harsh and unkind,
Yet under this eye, true peace we can find.

For every rise and fall, there's guidance above,
As light dances softly, a message of love.
In moments like these, we're never alone,
Together in silence, our spirits have grown.

With each breath we take, we trust in the way,
That leads us to futures filled with bright rays.
Under heaven's watch, we share what we sow,
A river of kindness forever will flow.

As day turns to night, with whispers of grace,
We gather our dreams, in this sacred space.
United forever, our hearts intertwined,
Under heaven's watchful eye, love is defined.

A Sanctuary of Spirits

In the hush of the forest, where shadows dance,
We gather as spirits, united by chance.
The rustle of leaves speaks a language so pure,
In this sacred place, we find our allure.

With every soft breeze, a prayer takes flight,
Echoes of laughter, our hearts feel the light.
Each moment reflected, the past and the now,
In the sanctuary's embrace, we humbly bow.

With eyes open wide, we share what we see,
The beauty around us, nature's decree.
With gratitude flowing in timeless embrace,
A sanctuary built on love's gentle grace.

Each spirit a candle, flickering bright,
In unity standing, we bask in the light.
Through trials we journey, and joys we proclaim,
Together we rise, forever the same.

As twilight descends, we whisper our dreams,
In this haven of peace, not all is as it seems.
With spirits in blossom, we claim our own part,
In this sanctuary of spirits, we find our true heart.

Communion of the Broken and Whole

In shadows cast by weary hearts,
We gather close, where love imparts.
In shared despair, we find our thread,
A tapestry from what we've shed.

Through tears that flow like rivers wide,
We learn to heal, we learn to bide.
In sacred space, we lift our plea,
For in the broken, whole we've seen.

Together now, we stand as one,
Beneath the gaze of setting sun.
With every wound, a story told,
In faith, our spirits will unfold.

We break the bread, our hands entwined,
In every crack, the light we find.
For in our flaws, God's grace does shine,
A union forged in love divine.

So let the chorus rise anew,
Of joy and pain, of me and you.
In every heart, a whisper's glow,
The communion of the broken, whole.

The Pilgrimage of Shared Journeys

We walk this path, the earth our guide,
In every step, our dreams collide.
Through mountains high and valleys deep,
In trust, we find the promises we keep.

Each stride we take, a tale to weave,
In borrowed moments, we believe.
With heavy hearts and weary feet,
Together, we make our journey sweet.

A sacred bond that ties our fate,
In kindness shared, we elevate.
Through whispered prayers and voices strong,
In unity, we all belong.

With open hands and lifted eyes,
We seek the truth that never lies.
In every soul, a spark divine,
In every heart, the light will shine.

Our pilgrimage, a dance of grace,
In every meeting, find a trace.
Of love that flows through time and space,
Together, we embrace this place.

In the Stillness, We Find Our Strength

In quietude, the spirit stirs,
A gentle breeze, a feathered whir.
In stillness deep, the heart does speak,
For in this void, we find what's meek.

With every breath, the silence calls,
As time bestows its gentle thralls.
We pause to hear the sacred sigh,
In tranquil moments, we rely.

The strength of calm, a well within,
In hushed embrace, we shed our sin.
With faith that blooms in shadow's light,
We rise anew, embraced by night.

With every heartbeat, grace unfolds,
In quiet spaces, truth beholds.
In woven silence lies our peace,
Where strife shall fade and worries cease.

So let us dwell in sacred hush,
In stillness deep, we know the rush.
With open hearts, we seek, we find,
In every pause, our souls aligned.

A Symphony of Souls Intertwined

In every note, a tale is sung,
A symphony where hearts are strung.
With voices raised to heavens high,
Together, we shall testify.

Through chords of faith and strings of grace,
We find our place in time and space.
With rhythms deep, our spirits dance,
In harmony, we take our chance.

Each soul a thread in vibrant hue,
Together strong, we weave anew.
In shared connection, love ignites,
A melody that soars and fights.

Through laughter's joy and sorrow's pain,
In every measure, we remain.
With hearts ablaze, the music swells,
In unity, our story tells.

So let the symphony resound,
In every heart, a sacred sound.
In intertwining, we are whole,
A masterpiece of every soul.

Lanterns of Love in the Dark

In the night where shadows creep,
Lanterns glow, their vigil keep.
Hearts entwined through faith and grace,
Guiding souls to a sacred place.

In whispers soft, love's light does shine,
Binding all with threads divine.
Through trials faced and burdens borne,
Together rise, new hope is sworn.

Each flicker tells of stories old,
Of love's warmth, a truth retold.
United strength, through storms we stand,
Lanterns held by loving hand.

In the darkness, light we share,
A beacon bright, with tender care.
For in our hearts, love's fire burns,
With every step, a new hope turns.

Together we will walk this path,
In love's embrace, we find our math.
Lanterns of love, forever bright,
Shining hope in darkest night.

The Well of Kindness Overflows

At the heart, a wellspring flows,
With gentle streams, compassion grows.
In kindness shared, the spirit blooms,
Lighting up the world, dispelling glooms.

With every drop, a seed is sown,
In the hearts of those alone.
From hands that give, and souls that care,
Together in this love we share.

Cupped in hands, from this well we drink,
Uniting hearts in tender links.
The laughter sparkles like the stream,
In kindness found, we find our dream.

For every tear that falls like rain,
The well restores; it heals the pain.
Compassion flows, a sacred pledge,
Through kindness, we live and hedge.

In every act of love we sow,
This precious well of kindness grows.
As voices rise in sweet refrain,
Together we break every chain.

Resonance of Faith in Togetherness

In silent halls where echoes dwell,
Resonates the sacred spell.
Joined in faith, we lift our song,
A harmony that makes us strong.

Each heart a note in timeless score,
In togetherness, we seek much more.
Voices blend, as spirits rise,
Together we touch the skies.

Through trials fierce, and shadows long,
The pulse of hope, a steadfast throng.
In unity, our faith will gleam,
Reflecting light, igniting dream.

Let every beat of heart declare,
In faith and love, we find our share.
Hand in hand, through every fight,
Together we embrace the light.

With every prayer, and every plea,
We weave the threads of destiny.
In the resonance of faith, we find,
A love unbound, eternally kind.

The Light of Kindness Illuminates

In the depths where shadows lie,
The light of kindness lifts us high.
With gentle hands that soothe the pain,
We bloom anew, like summer rain.

Each smile shared, a glimmer bright,
Guiding souls through darkest night.
In kindness' name, we bind our fates,
Opening wide affection's gates.

With every act of love we show,
Compassion's fire begins to grow.
Illuminating paths once lost,
A beacon found, however tossed.

Together, strong, we face the dawn,
With kindness' light, we're never gone.
Through winding roads, we find our way,
In every heart, it's here to stay.

So let us walk with hearts aligned,
In this light, our souls entwined.
For kindness shines, forever true,
A gift we share, in all we do.

The Sacred Tapestry of Hearts

In whispers soft, the spirits weave,
Threads of love, in silence cleave.
Each soul a stitch, in divine design,
Together they flow, in love's sweet line.

Through trials faced, our hearts align,
With faith as our guide, all souls entwine.
In every tear, and every smile,
The sacred tapestry spans each mile.

In quiet prayers, our hopes take flight,
Illuminating paths, with grace and light.
A fervent bond, in joy and strife,
In Christ's embrace, we find our life.

We cherish each soul, in the sacred fold,
A story beloved, eternally told.
With hands uplifted, we seek to bless,
This tapestry rich, in holiness.

In unity's strength, we rise and stand,
Anointed by love, united, we band.
With open hearts, we seek to impart,
The sacred truth that lives in our hearts.

Gathering in the Radiance of Hope

Beneath the heavens, bright stars align,
We gather together, our spirits combine.
In the warmth of community, hope ignites,
Guiding us gently through darkest nights.

Each soul, a beacon of light to share,
In laughter and tears, we find solace there.
With faith intertwined, we soar above,
Locked in a bond, woven through love.

In moments of doubt, when shadows fall,
We lift one another, answering the call.
With hearts wide open, we cherish the gift,
In the radiance of hope, our spirits uplift.

Like flowers in bloom, we flourish and grow,
United in purpose, we'll never lose hope.
With gratitude clear, we walk hand in hand,
In the warmth of our gathering, we'll forever stand.

Through trials and storms, our faith won't shake,
In the embrace of love, there's no heartache.
Together we'll rise, in the light so bright,
Gathering in hope, as one in the light.

Celestial Bonds of Understanding

In the silence of prayer, we find our way,
Binding our hearts in the light of the day.
Celestial whispers, guiding our flight,
Through valleys of darkness to shimmering light.

With eyes that see beyond surface skins,
In every story, the journey begins.
We listen with grace, for wisdom to flow,
In the warmth of connection, our love will grow.

Together we seek, what the spirit can teach,
In the depths of our souls, our hearts will reach.
Empathy's touch creates bonds that endure,
In the vastness of understanding, our love will secure.

Through trials we face, we'll rise as one,
In unity's light, our work is begun.
With open arms, we embrace the divine,
Celestial bonds, forever entwined.

In every heartbeat, we cherish the ties,
That weave through our spirits, like stars in the skies.
With eyes wide open, and hearts that embrace,
In celestial bonds, we find our place.

In the Garden of Kindness Blooms

In the garden of life, where kindness thrives,
Each act of love, a flower that strives.
With gentle hands, we sow and we share,
Each moment of grace, a fragrant prayer.

Beneath the sun's glow, our hearts take flight,
Nurtured by hope, we bask in its light.
In the soil of faith, our dreams take root,
In the garden of kindness, compassion bears fruit.

Through storms that may come, we hold each other,
In the embrace of grace, all are sister and brother.
With petals of mercy, we blossom anew,
In a tapestry woven, our love shines through.

Together we walk, through life's winding maze,
In giving and sharing, we find endless praise.
In the garden of kindness, our spirits entwine,
With each thoughtful gesture, our hearts align.

So let us cultivate joy, foster peace,
In this sacred garden, let kindness increase.
For in love we find what our hearts have known,
In the garden of kindness, we are never alone.

Milton Keynes UK
Ingram Content Group UK Ltd.
UKHW020037271124
451585UK00012B/910